It's Not What It Looks Like

Experiencing Victory in the Face of Adversity

Calvin M. Hooper

Table of Contents

Unless otherwise noted, all scripture references are from
the NASB and NKJV version

Introduction

This book is derived from the story of the Israelites in Exodus 14. The Israelites had been in Egypt for a long time. How did they get there? If we briefly recap some events of scripture we will see that they went there voluntarily. In the book of Genesis, the story of Joseph is told. Joseph was sold into slavery by his brothers. Joseph ended up in Egypt and ascended to the second highest political office in the land. Only Pharaoh was higher than Joseph. When famine struck in Israel, Joseph's brothers went to Egypt to search for food. They had no idea that the one who would literally save their life was the brother they thought they would never see again, Joseph. Joseph's father Jacob already thought he was dead, but Joseph and his brothers reconciled with one another and they and Jacob, their father, all moved to Egypt. At this point it seems like the story has a happy ending but in Genesis 15:13 (NKJV) God told Abraham, Jacob's grandfather... ***"Know certainly that your descendants will be strangers in a land that is not theirs, and will serve them, and they will afflict them four hundred years.***

The Israelites multiplied greatly in Egypt and everything seemed to be fine until a new king rose to power in Egypt. Exodus 1:8-13 (NKJV) says... ***Now there arose a*** *new king over Egypt, who did not know Joseph. And he said to his people, "Look, the people of the children of Israel are more and mightier than we; "come, let us deal shrewdly with them, lest they multiply, and it happen, in the event of war, that they also join our enemies and fight against us, and so go up out of the land." Therefore, they set taskmasters over them to afflict them with their burdens. And they built for Pharaoh supply cities, Pithom and Raamses. But the more they afflicted them, the more they multiplied and grew. And they were in dread of the children of Israel. So the Egyptians made the children of Israel serve with rigor.*

Therefore, the children of Israel were in bondage to the Egyptians for hundreds of years just as God had told Abraham. However, that is not the end of the story because God also told Abraham in Genesis 15:14 (NKJV)... *"And also, the nation whom they serve I will judge; afterward they shall come out with great possessions.*

After a series of plagues in the land, which are detailed in the book of Exodus, the Lord delivered them out of the hands of the Egyptians like He said He would. They didn't just leave, but according to Exodus 12:35-36 they left with much gold, silver, and clothing. It's good to know we serve a God that keeps His promises! Life can present us with many challenges and tests. Oftentimes, we lose focus of the God we serve because we are so impacted by the situation at hand. What we must always remember is that God is ever present and whatever He has promised, He will perform. When we maintain the proper focus, we will see things as we should because we know that no matter how dire the situation, it's not what it looks like. Be encouraged!

Chapter One
The Response of the Enemy

Exodus 14 tells the story of what happened after he Israelites had been released from bondage in Egypt. When the enemy considered what had happened they questioned themselves as to why they let the people go. At the time that Pharaoh told them to leave, it sounded like a great idea since there was not an Egyptian household where the first born of both man and beast were not dead after God fulfilled the promise He made in Exodus 12:5-13. It says...

Your lamb shall be an unblemished male a year old; you may take it from the sheep or from the goats. You shall keep it until the fourteenth day of the same month, then the whole assembly of the congregation of Israel is to kill it at twilight. Moreover, they shall take some of the blood and put it on the two doorposts and on the lintel of the houses in which they eat it. They shall eat the flesh that same night, roasted with fire, and they shall eat it with unleavened bread and bitter herbs. Do not eat any of it raw or boiled at all with water, but rather roasted with fire, both its head and its legs along with its entrails. and you shall not leave any of it over until morning, but whatever is left of it until morning, you shall burn with fire. Now you shall eat it in this manner: with your loins girded, your sandals on your feet, and your staff in your hand; and you shall eat it in haste- it is the Lord's Passover. For I will go through the land of Egypt on that night, and will strike down all the firstborn in the land of Egypt, both man and beast; and against all the gods of Egypt I will execute judgments-I am the Lord. The blood shall be a sign for you on the houses where you live; and when I see the blood I will pass over you, and no plague will befall you to destroy you when I strike the land of Egypt.

Initially, all that Pharaoh wanted after God fulfilled His promise, was for the Israelites to leave as quickly as possible. It probably hadn't sunk in yet that it was ultimately God, not him, that was setting the captives free. After they were released from bondage in Egypt, Pharaoh had a change of heart and gathered his men together to go after the Israelites, with the intent to bring them back to serve them.

Now here are the Israelites, on their journey, and unbeknownst to them, the enemy is planning an attack to spoil their blessing. Most were probably happy that after 400 hard years of slavery to the Egyptians they were free. Some were probably skeptical about it since the only thing they knew was being in bondage. Nevertheless, this was essentially a new beginning. This was a breakthrough. They were able to live their lives free from the oppression of Pharaoh and the Egyptians.

However, the enemy, Pharaoh, was not happy at all about their new-found freedom and he was locked in on doing something about it. The enemy is not happy when we get blessed either and he is intent on robbing us of our joy, killing our happiness, and he ultimately wants to keep us underachieving in our faith by using fear, and casting doubt to make you believe he has the upper hand, but we have to remember, that the Lord will fight our battles if we trust Him! Pharaoh didn't just gather any old guys together. In addition to his chariot, verse 7 says... ***Also, he took six hundred choice chariots, and all the chariots of Egypt with captains over every one of them.*** If this were happening today, it would be like the finest military tanks coming after them! Pharaoh was bringing some serious heat on them!

The devil, likewise, always tries to give us his best shot, but when we trust in the Lord, every attempt he brings will amount to nothing and we will see our blessing manifest! However, although God brought the Israelites out of Egypt, they apparently got amnesia as soon as they saw Pharaoh's army coming! Does that sound like us sometimes? As soon as we see the enemy raising his head a little bit, we forget all that God has done for us in the past! The same God that brought you out before is still able to bring you out now! Let's look at their reaction.

Notes_____

_____

_____

_____

_____

_____

_____

_____

_____

_____

_____

_____

_____

_____

_____

_____

_____

_____

_____

_____

_____

_____

Chapter Two

The Reaction of the People

When the people saw Pharaoh's army coming, their hearts literally melted and they did several things. You could call this a list of THINGS NOT TO DO WHEN THE ENEMY IS ON YOUR TRAIL!!! One thing they did which was good, was they prayed to God. It wasn't a prayer of faith, but a prayer of panic motivated by things they should not have done such as...

1. They got scared!

To them it looked like the end of the road. It looked like freedom was over. This is the same thing that happens to people today. As soon as something disrupts the peace in our life, fear sets in for many people! Whether it's a job loss, health challenge, financial difficulty, family struggle, or one of many other things, along comes fear. Christians really have no need to fear, so our fear is really without any basis. **Paul told Timothy in 2 Timothy 1:7 "God has not given us a Spirit of Fear but of power, love and a sound mind.**

A Japanese soldier by the name of Shoichi Yokoi lived in a cave on the island of Guam to which he fled in 1944 when the tides of war began to change. Fearing for his life, this man stayed hidden for twenty-eight years in the jungle cave, coming out only at night. During this long period of time, this self-imposed hermit lived on frogs, rats, snails, shrimp, nuts, and mangoes. He had carried a pair of trousers and a jacket from a burlap like cloth made from tree bark. Yokoi said that he knew the war was over because of leaflets that were scattered throughout the jungles of Guam. But he was afraid that if he came out of hiding, he would be executed. Finally, two hunters came upon him and told him that he need not hide any longer. At last he was free, and with new clothes to wear and food to eat, he was taken by plane to his home. —*Carl C. Williams*

Considering all that God had done for them, the Israelites, just like Shoichi Yokoi, had no reason to fear, but that's what fear can do. It can get your focus off what God has done and can do, and make you get caught up in the moment, making the imminence of the moment seem greater than the matchless power of almighty God! Even though God's presence was right there in the form of the pillar of cloud by day and fire by night as it says in Exodus 13:21, they were afraid. Even though His presence didn't leave them because of trouble on the horizon, they were still afraid! We all can become victims of fear at any given stage of our life, but we don't have to fear when we are in the presence of God! Psalm 91:1-8 says... *He who dwells in the shelter of the Most High will abide in the shadow of the Almighty. I will say to the Lord, "My refuge and my fortress, My God, in whom I trust!" For it is He who delivers you from the snare of the trapper and from the deadly pestilence. He will cover you with His pinions, and under His wings you may seek refuge; His faithfulness is a shield and bulwark. You will not be afraid of the terror by night, or of the arrow that flies by day; of the pestilence that stalks in darkness, or of the destruction that lays waste at noon. A thousand may fall at your side and ten thousand at your right hand, but it shall not approach you. You will only look on with your eyes and see the recompense of the wicked.*

I want you to also take note that this was all **ALLOWED BY GOD for HIS GLORY**! Pharaoh's army coming after them wasn't because of a bad decision they made, it wasn't because of disobedience, and it wasn't about anything they did. It was simply for God's glory! They didn't understand why this was happening, but God had a plan. **In your life, there are things that will happen that you won't understand, but just know that God knows and He has allowed it for His glory! It may not feel comfortable, but when it's over you'll be able to testify of what God has done!**

2. They started complaining to Moses.

When they saw the enemy coming, and after they started crying out to God, they said to Moses... *"Because there were no graves in Egypt, have you taken us away to die in the wilderness? Why have you so dealt with us, to bring us up out of Egypt?* In other words, "Hey Moses, we could have died back in Egypt man!" "Why are you treating your people like this?" Imagine the pressure Moses must have felt as complaints are being hurled at him from this massive group of people. Exodus 12 beginning with verse 37 gives us some insight on the size of this group. It says...

Then the children of Israel journeyed from Rameses to Succoth, about six hundred thousand men on foot, besides children. A mixed multitude went up with them also, and flocks and herds--a great deal of livestock.

Imagine how God must feel when we complain to Him in the face of a pressure situation even after He has already proven to us that He is able to deliver. God wants us to be thankful! It's not because everything we face is pleasant, or because everything we face is allowed by God for His glory. In fact, many things we face in life are the direct result of our own choices, but when we invite God into whatever the situation is, He can work it out. Two scriptures came to mind when I thought about the will of God and His power to deliver. The first is 1 Thessalonians 5:18 which says... *in everything give thanks; for this is the will of God in Christ Jesus for you.* The second almost sounds like the reason you should give thanks at it is Romans 8:28 (NKJV) which says... *And we know that all things work together for good to those who love God, to those who are the called according to His purpose.* The Israelites did pray when the situation arose, but they had a fear driven prayer rather than a faith driven prayer. Here is something to remember: **God is not obligated to respond to fear, He responds to faith!**

3. They started playing the blame game.

After they launched their share of complaints at Moses, they started the blame game. In Exodus 14:12 they *said "Is this not the word that we told you in Egypt, saying, 'Let us alone that we may serve the Egyptians'? For it would have been better for us to serve the Egyptians than that we should die in the wilderness."* They basically told Moses, "See, I told you so! We should have stayed in Egypt. At least we'd have a safe place to stay and wouldn't have Pharaoh's army pursuing after us! How are we supposed to get out of this mess Moses? This is all your fault!" Likewise, we can be guilty of the blame game. As soon as things go in a direction we judge as wrong, we start trying to find who or what to blame for our situation. Husbands blame wives, wives blame husbands, children blame parents, employees blame employers, employers blame employees, and more. Rather than blame anyone, go to God in prayer! His word tells us in Philippians 4:6-7...

Be anxious for nothing, but in everything by prayer and supplication, with thanksgiving, let your requests be made known to God; and the peace of God, which surpasses all understanding, will guard your hearts and minds through Christ Jesus.

We have seen the response of the enemy to their release, and the reaction of the people to the sight of Pharaoh's men, but Moses, instead of retaliating against the people, he reassured the people that everything would be just fine.

Notes_____

_____

_____

_____

_____

_____

_____

_____

_____

_____

_____

_____

_____

_____

_____

_____

_____

_____

_____

_____

_____

_____

Chapter Three

The Reassurance of Moses

Moses told the people *"Do not be afraid. Stand still, and see the salvation of the LORD, which He will accomplish for you today. For the Egyptians whom you see today, you shall see again no more forever. "The LORD will fight for you, and you shall hold your peace."* That meant stop your complaining, stop your blaming, stop trying to ponder your options for how you are going to handle this and hold fast to faith in God. Watch God work out your situation. Watch God turn nothing into something and something into nothing. Watch God open a door that others said could not be opened. Watch God move on your behalf!

I love the question that God asked Moses in verse 15. He said... *"Why do you cry to Me?* Then He said...*Tell the children of Israel to go forward.* God is saying the same thing to people today which is basically, why are you still praying about what I already told you I was going to do? There is a time for prayer, and there is a time for action! This was a time for action for the Israelites, and for some of us, it may be a time of action! When we pray we also should listen for God to answer us. When He gives the answer, it's not time to keep praying about the same thing, it is time to act! It's kind of like being in school and being given a clearly stated assignment by the teacher and then repeatedly asking them, is this what you want me to do? Maybe God has given you an assignment to launch out in the deep and start a new career or business. It's not time to pray and ask God if that's what He wants you to do, it's time to act! Maybe God has assigned you to be a blessing to someone that you may or may not know has a need. It's not time to pray about it, it's time to act! Maybe God has called you into the ministry, but you keep praying about it. It's not time to pray about it, God has already told you what to do, so now it's time to... ACT!!! Moses told them the Lord would accomplish the victory not next week, next month or next year, but today!

Many times, we are on the verge of seeing the manifestation of a blessing from the Lord, but we have to stand still and see the salvation of the Lord. God was going to make this fight so utterly complete for the Israelites that they would see this enemy no more forever! Just as God gave Moses the words to share with the people to reassure them everything would be fine, we can find that same assurance in the Word of God today. Psalm 37:5 says

Commit your way to the LORD, Trust also in Him, And He shall bring it to pass.

The problem for many Christians is that they are busy trying to provide solutions instead of giving their situations to the solution provider. When we do this, we remain anxious, stressed out, restless, but when we resolve in our minds to trust God we can rest in the peace of God and know that He will handle whatever it is.

Notes_____

_____

_____

_____

_____

_____

_____

_____

_____

_____

_____

_____

_____

_____

_____

_____

_____

_____

_____

_____

_____

_____

_____

_____

Chapter Four

The Restatement of the Promise

Here are the Israelites in a land that is not theirs that they have served 400 plus years of hard labor in, and they have a serious dilemma. They had reason to be happy because of their release from bondage, but here comes the enemy to crash the party. When the children of Israel saw the army of Pharaoh coming they had the wrong reaction. In Exodus 14:10 the Bible says...

And when Pharaoh drew near, the children of Israel lifted their eyes, and behold, the Egyptians marched after them. So, they were very afraid, and the children of Israel cried out to the LORD.

Rather than reflecting on what God did to bring them out of their previous situation, they focused on the situation at hand and fear set in. That's how we still do today. When difficult situations arise many times, people go right into panic mode. The situation invites memories of the past hurt, pain, failure, difficulty, and struggles, instead of memories of what God did to bring you through the hurt, pain, failure, difficulty and struggles. As Christians, we need to be delivered from what I call the faithless reflection mode and into faithful reflection mode. What is the difference? Faithless reflection means that when situations arise that are difficult, we start reflecting on the difficult situations of the past and the *experience* we had *__while in it__*. In faithful reflection mode, we focus on the *exodus,* or the experience of coming out from those difficult situations of the past, and *God who was in it*! God brought them out! I like the route He had them take to come out too. The Bible declares to us in Exodus 13:17...

__Then it came to pass, when Pharaoh had let the people go, that God did not lead them by way of the land of the Philistines, although that was near;__ for God said, "Lest perhaps the people change their minds when they see war, and return to Egypt."

In other words, they did not take the most logical, most convenient way; they took the route that they would not have taken if it were up to them. That scripture says to me that just like they went through territory that was not the closest route, that sometimes we may have to go through some things that may not be convenient or make sense to us, but God has a plan and a purpose for it to help lead us to our destiny!

The Israelites were camped out near the Red Sea, the enemy was approaching from behind, they started complaining to Moses and pointing blame at him, they felt trapped with nowhere to go and then God spoke again to Moses.

Let's refresh our memory on what Moses said to the people after they knew the enemy was coming and they began to complain to and point blame at Moses. He said in Exodus 14:13-14... *And Moses said to the people, "Do not be afraid. Stand still, and see the salvation of the LORD, which He will accomplish for you today. For the Egyptians whom you see today, you shall see again no more forever. "The LORD will fight for you, and you shall hold your peace."*

He told them what not to do, when he said **do not be afraid**. He told them what to do, which was **stand still**. Then he told them what they should expect to see **(the salvation of the Lord),** he acknowledged what they currently saw **(the Egyptians),** and he told them what they wouldn't see any more **(the Egyptians).** After he spoke to the people, God spoke to him. There are three main things to note about what was said.

1. God gave Moses further instructions

After Moses addressed the people with words of comfort and encouragement, and before that historic Red Sea crossing took place, God told him to lift his rod and stretch out his hand over the sea and divide it! Now, this was going to require Moses to have faith. The rod in and of itself was not able to actually divide the water, but by faith, Moses was going to have to lift it up in order to see the promise of God manifest. God is a God of order. He gave Moses **(1) INSTRUCTIONS** and **(2) A PROMISE**!

Many times, in the word of God we are given instructions that if followed will cause the promised blessing to manifest. In Philippians 4:6 we are given instructions (*be anxious for nothing*...), in Philippians 4:7 we have the promise (...*and the peace of God...will guard your hearts and minds*). In Malachi 3:10 says to bring all the tithes into the storehouse (**those are instructions**). Malachi 3:10-11 tells us God will pour out blessing that we won't have room enough to receive, and more (**that's a promise**). So Moses, with rod in hand was going to have to exercise his faith! The Bible in James 2:17 tells us that faith without works is dead! Moses did not have time to reflect on how messed up the situation they were in was. He did not have time to cry about their predicament. He did not have time to sit and reminisce with the people on the time they had in Egypt, or even to consider what if this lifting of the rod idea doesn't work. God told him what to do, and now the time was at hand!

Many of us want to see God's blessings manifest, but even after God has spoken to us whether it's through the pages of His word, through the preached word of God or another way, we don't act. Why? Because we get too caught up in the moment that we lose momentum! We get too caught up in the situation and start asking questions like, why am I in this situation, Lord (**answer: because you're not exempt and perhaps so you'll learn to trust God and not self**), or, when is God going to bring us out of this (**answer: when you stop going back and forth between faith and doubt and consistently act in faith**).

2. God told Moses exactly what would happen

God said...*And the children of Israel shall go on dry ground through the midst of the sea.* It had to blow Moses mind that God was going to give them a dry path through water. At that point many Christians would ask, "Well how is that going to happen, God". They would say, "We can't go through the water and stay dry! That doesn't make sense! What do you mean God?" I can think of so many times in my life that I've been required of God to do some things that did not line up with my human reasoning and logic, but every single time I obeyed God, He always showed me that He knows best. Why? Because the Bible says...

"For My thoughts are not your thoughts, Nor are your ways My ways," says the LORD. "For as the heavens are higher than the earth, so are My ways higher than your ways, and My thoughts than your thoughts. (Isa 55:8-9)

The more time we spend asking God questions about things He already has figured out, the more time we waste getting to the blessing He has waiting! The third aspect of God's restatement of the promise was that He reminded Moses of what He said before.

3. God reminded him of what He would do for them

He told him in Exodus 14:17...*"And I indeed will harden the hearts of the Egyptians, and they shall follow them. So I will gain honor over Pharaoh and over all his army, his chariots, and his horsemen.* Many times God has to remind us of what He will do, has done, can do etc.!!! Many times people get stuck in the past and it causes them to stop moving forward. However, the only part of our past we need to look back and dwell on from time to time is *the faithfulness of God to bring us to where we are now*!

It's funny how quickly we forget the words of God in the latter part of Hebrews 13:5 which says... *For He Himself has said, "I will never leave you nor forsake you."* I know when we face difficulty in life that it can sometimes seem like we are all alone, but no matter what we go through, we are NEVER ALONE!

The enemy was behind the Israelites, the sea was in front of them, and they had nowhere to go but forward. I'm sure they were trying to figure out which way to go, but they could not turn around and fight the enemy in their own power, they could not take an alternate route along the seashore; they had to follow Moses, They had to believe that God was as faithful now as He was in the past, and go through it! God restated the promise to Moses, but before they could move forward and have considerable progress they had to get refocused.

Notes_____

_____

_____

_____

_____

_____

_____

_____

_____

_____

_____

_____

_____

_____

_____

_____

_____

_____

_____

_____

Chapter Five

Refocused on the Presence of God

Verse 19-20 says...***And the Angel of God, who went before the camp of Israel, moved and went behind them; and the pillar of cloud went from before them and stood behind them. So it came between the camp of the Egyptians and the camp of Israel. Thus it was a cloud and darkness to the one, and it gave light by night to the other, so that the one did not come near the other all that night.***

The first thing we need to address so we will understand the following points is who the Angel of God is. According to the book, Hard Sayings of the Bible...

Many Old Testament passages state that this angel is God. Thus, after being told that Hagar had been speaking with the angel of the Lord (four times in Gen 16:7, 9-11), Genesis 16:13 informs us that Hagar "gave this name to the LORD who spoke to her: `You are the God who sees me.'" Jacob's testimony in Genesis 48:15-16 is even more striking. He identifies the God in whose presence his father's Abraham and Isaac had lived as "the God who has been my shepherd all my life to this day, the Angel who has delivered me from all harm."

This angel spoke to Jacob earlier in a dream and identified himself by saying, "I am the God of Bethel, where you anointed a pillar and where you made a vow to me" (Gen 31:11, 13).

Likewise in Exodus 3:2-6 the phrase "the angel of the LORD" is used interchangeably with "the LORD." In fact the angel claims, "I am the God of your father, the God of Abraham, the God of Isaac and the God of Jacob" (Ex 3:6).

The passage, however, that really clinches this remarkable identification is Exodus 23:20-23. There God promises to send his angel ahead of the children of Israel as they go through the desert. The Israelites were warned that they must obey and not rebel against this angel. The reason was a stunning one: "Since my Name is in him." God would never share his memorial name with anyone else; for Isaiah 42:8 advised that he would never share his glory with another. Thus the name of God stands for himself. And when a person is said to have the name of God in him, that person is God!

The Angel of God was a preincarnate appearance of Christ! The Angel of God repositioned Himself from in front of them to behind them along with the pillar of cloud. What we can see here is...

1. They needed their focus readjusted

In verse 10, we see that the Israelites fixed their eyes on the Egyptians and then we do not see them look towards anything else until they had no choice to when the Angel of God repositioned Himself. He got between their enemy and them. Now, if they looked back, the presence of God could be seen there. If they looked forward, they would see the presence of God there in what God was about to do. Sometimes our biggest problem is a lack of proper focus. We can make even the smallest thing seem so big and so bad that we can't focus on anything else. What we need to do is told to us in Hebrews 12:2. We need to keep... *looking unto Jesus, the author and finisher of our faith...*

2. The Angel of God and the Pillar got behind them for protection

He was their protection. The enemy came after them still, but could not catch up to them. The pillar of cloud was darkness to them, but light to the Israelites. When you are in the dark, it's much more difficult to move forward for fear of the fact you may run into something, trip over something, fall, etc. The Egyptians with their fine horses and chariots could not make up any ground on the Israelites because their vision was impaired. Remember, they are on war horses and chariots; the Israelites are for the most part on foot. They had over 600 thousand people, livestock, gold, silver, and clothing but although they were traveling at night, they were in the light. They could see their way. This well-oiled Egyptian army could not make up any ground because God kept them in the dark! The same thing happens to us. When God blesses us, our enemy the devil, desires to overtake us with his devices but if we keep trusting God, he won't make up any ground on us. We seem to sometimes think that the devil has power that is along the same level as God, but that's not the case. Only God is Omnipotent, only God is Omniscient, only God is Omnipresent. The devil may look like he has the upper hand in your life sometimes, but he's, in essence, operating in the dark. What he doesn't know is the fate his plan shall meet just a little further down the road! If the Egyptians knew what they were about to experience, they would have called off the attack and headed back home as fast as possible!

3. The Angel of God had their back!

He was protecting them. We need to stop worrying about what the enemy is trying to scheme against us and know that God is working it out! I believe God was sending them a message that the same God that went before you is the same God that has your back. That's a message we need to embrace! The same God that has been making a way before you is the same God that has your back, He's working behind the scenes, even when it may seem like He's forgotten about you, and His plan is still at work! As long as they had their eyes on the enemy, their concern would be more about what the enemy **might do** than what God **can do**! So this repositioning was a way of saying I've got you covered. I've got you covered in from the front, back, all around, and you don't have to worry about the enemy, I'll handle them! Psalm 37 says...

Do not fret because of evildoers, Nor be envious of the workers of iniquity For they shall soon be cut down like the grass, And wither as the green herb.

You can't move forward until you stop looking back! Refocus and reclaim the path to your destiny!

Notes_____

Chapter Six

The Revelation of Another Miracle

Now that God has refocused them, there is no reason for them to stay in that place, now it's time to exercise faith and move. What they would experience as they do is the revelation of another miracle.

The Israelites had already been witnesses to God's miracle working power before. In fact, each of the ten plagues that descended upon the land of Egypt was miraculous. However, the tenth plague was one that brought about the release from captivity in Egypt. That was the one that really got Pharaoh's attention. The Bible says in Exodus 12:29-31...

And it came to pass at midnight that the LORD struck all the firstborn in the land of Egypt, from the firstborn of Pharaoh who sat on his throne to the firstborn of the captive who was in the dungeon, and all the firstborn of livestock. So Pharaoh rose in the night, he, all his servants, and all the Egyptians; and there was a great cry in Egypt, for there was not a house where there was not one dead. Then he called for Moses and Aaron by night, and said, "Rise, go out from among my people, both you and the children of Israel. And go, serve the LORD as you have said.

Now they are on the verge of seeing another miracle. The situation had no way out BUT God was about to make a way!!! Sometimes we can experience situations that seem to have no way out but God makes a way every time! God's methods may not make sense to us, but when we are walking by faith and not sight, we have to trust God with every aspect of our life. Moses has already received his instructions from God. There was nothing else to be discussed. He couldn't try to bargain with God or cut a deal with Him. Now is the moment of truth!

God told Moses to lift the rod and divide the sea. We have already come to the conclusion and reality that the rod in and of itself could not divide the water, but this is the process God told Moses to follow to see the miracle come to pass.

Let me reiterate an earlier point that God is a God of order. *First,* Moses had to lift the rod, **AND THEN** the sea would part. In our Christian walk we are required to lift something to God first in order to see blessings manifest, and it's called prayer. We are motivated to pray because of our FAITH in God. We don't pray **to** have faith, we pray **because** we have faith. We live by faith, not by sight. We are told in 1 Thessalonians 5:17 to pray without ceasing. That doesn't mean that we spend every waking moment of our time on Earth in prayer, it simply means that we have a level of consistency in our prayer life. For example, a person may say, "I go to church all the time." We would be mistaken to think the person is saying that they literally spend all of their time in church, but we would be correct if we understood them to mean that they went to church on a regular basis. When we pray in faith, we can please God. When we pray without faith we cannot please God. Hebrews 11:6 says...

But without faith it is impossible to please Him, for he who comes to God must believe that He is, and that He is a rewarder of those who diligently seek Him.

Once we pray in faith we also must act in faith. When you've seen God move before, your level of faith is increased and you know that if God did it for you before, He's able to do it again. Faith comes as a result of the word of God. Romans 10:17 says... ***So then faith comes by hearing, and hearing by the word of God.*** So it basically goes like this, we hear the WORD and that builds our FAITH. Because of our FAITH we PRAY. As a result of our praying and then acting in FAITH, God moves on our behalf, and that causes our FAITH to be strengthened which in turn, motivates us to keep praying. It is safe to assume that Moses because of his experience and what he had witnessed as leader of the people must have had faith in God. Moses proceeded to lift his rod and when he did the Bible in Exodus 14: 21 lets us know that God, not Moses, divided the sea.

When the sea divided, the Israelites moved forward and the Egyptians followed them. The fact that the Egyptians followed them is an amazing thing to me for several reasons.

1. **The first born in Egypt died on the night of the Passover.** It seems like they would have acknowledged the power of God and left Israel alone.

2. **The Red Sea parted**. It seems like that would have caused them to acknowledge the power of God.

3. **They were going through the Red Sea on dry ground.** Surely this had to get their attention!

No matter what, the Egyptians were determined to get the Israelites!!! They remind me of how the devil is. The devil is a defeated foe, but no matter what, he's always trying to scheme something against you. He just doesn't know when to quit! It would seem as though the Egyptians would have retreated when they saw the Red Sea had parted since they had to know that the Israelites did not possess the power in and of themselves to perform such a feat. God's people followed Moses, stood still, trusted God, held their peace and walked into their blessing. I noticed that earlier in the 14th chapter, the Israelites were afraid, complaining, and pointing blame at Moses for their situation, thinking that they were surely going to perish at the hands of the Egyptians, but as we see them now, they weren't hurt, captured, killed, didn't have to fight at all, they just walked into the blessing prepared for them. I believe someone right now has been standing still, trusting God, holding their peace and God is about to make the way for you to walk right in to your blessing! The Israelites didn't focus on the enemy; they just kept moving forward. When God has set you in the right direction, don't divert your attention on what the enemy may be doing, stay focused on what God is doing for you and keep moving forward!

As the Israelites were moving forward, the Egyptians with their mighty men of war, their horses and chariots ran into a bit of a dilemma themselves. Exodus 14:24-25 says…

Now it came to pass, in the morning watch, that the LORD looked down upon the army of the Egyptians through the pillar of fire and cloud, and He troubled the army of the Egyptians. And He took off their chariot wheels, so that they drove them with difficulty; and the Egyptians said, "Let us flee from the face of Israel, for the LORD fights for them against the Egyptians."

The Lord looked down on the enemy! The Lord never looks up at the enemy, so no matter how tough the situation, your help is coming from a ***HIGHER POWER***! God's eyes are always on the situation! 1 Peter 3:12 says… ***For the eyes of the LORD are on the righteous, and His ears are open to their prayers; But the face of the LORD is against those who do evil."***

Moses already told the people that the Lord would fight their battle, and as promised He did! Of course, it turned out not to be much of a battle at all. It was kind of like those old Mike Tyson fights where people paid $50 or more for the pay per view broadcast only to see Tyson annihilate his opponent in 20 seconds! Notice God didn't break out His chariots and fight Pharaoh's army chariot for chariot, He just looked down and ***TOOK THE WHEELS OFF THE CHARIOTS!***

The Egyptians then realized they had a problem. They said... ***"Let us flee from the face of Israel, for the LORD fights for them against the Egyptians."*** Since the pillar of cloud was still between the Israelites and the Egyptians, the Israelites may not have even been aware yet of what happened. God was taking care of the business of silencing the enemy for them while they took care of moving forward to the next stop, and they would realize later exactly what God had done. Suddenly, it dawned on the Egyptians that they better leave these people alone! They were messing with the wrong people!

This reminded me of an incident my family and I witnessed in downtown Austin , TX one day years ago. We were driving through Austin and got slightly delayed in downtown traffic. We saw a group of men having a heated discussion outside. One man and his friend tried to walk away to diffuse the situation, but the other group, with their ringleader, kept pushing the issue and kept pursuing after them. They did not have the sense to leave the situation alone. It wasn't until the man who was being followed whipped out a large meat cleaver like blade and started waving it around at the other man and shouted, *"You better leave me alone boy, you better leave me alone!* In our text, it was as if God was saying to the Egyptians, when He took off the chariot wheels, *"You better leave my people alone boys, you better leave them alone!"* God totally derailed the plans of the enemy!

We no longer have the pillar of cloud and the pillar of fire leading us like the Israelites had, but we have the same God and He has given us a weapon! A modernistic preacher announced in defending his liberal theological position, "I'm not afraid of the Devil." "That is not what matters so much," one of his acquaintances replied. "Let me ask you a more important question: Is the Devil afraid of you?"

In your life when the enemy launches his attacks, you can whip out your sword, which is the word of God, and start speaking the word of God over every life situation and when the devil sees you standing on the word of God, just like the Israelites had to stand on the word of God, He will realize, just like the Egyptians did, that it's time to retreat, God is fighting their battle, we better leave them alone! When you put your faith and trust in God's word, He will derail the plans of the enemy. Isaiah 59:19 says...*When the enemy comes in like a flood, The Spirit of the LORD will lift up a standard against him.*

The Lord set the enemy up for the knockout punch! He told Moses... ***"Stretch out your hand over the sea that the waters may come back upon the Egyptians, on their chariots, and on their horsemen." And Moses stretched out his hand over the sea; and when the morning appeared, the sea returned to its full depth, while the Egyptians were fleeing into it. So the LORD overthrew the Egyptians in the midst of the sea.***

It was too late for the Egyptians to get to safety. Soon, the Israelites would realize that victory was theirs!

Notes_____

_____

_____

_____

_____

_____

_____

_____

_____

_____

_____

_____

_____

_____

_____

_____

_____

_____

_____

_____

_____

Chapter 7

The Realization of Victory

Exodus 14: 30-31 says...

So the LORD saved Israel that day out of the hand of the Egyptians, and Israel saw the Egyptians dead on the seashore. Thus Israel saw the great work which the LORD had done in Egypt; so the people feared the LORD, and believed the LORD and His servant Moses.

When they saw the Egyptians dead on the seashore, it made me think about the fact that although they were troubled when they initially saw the Egyptians coming, TROUBLE didn't last ALWAYS. Some of the Egyptians finally caught up to the Israelites, but they weren't alive, they were dead on the seashore, and it was only to validate what God had done and to give Him the glory He deserved. The Egyptians were now officially a non-issue!

Job 14:1 says *"Man who is born of woman is of few days and full of trouble.* In your life, you will have trouble, but trouble doesn't last always. When you stand on God's word you can rest assured and know that your morning time is coming when everything will be clear and you'll see how God worked in your favor! You'll suddenly realize how God was hearing your prayers and working things out for you behind the scenes as you kept pushing forward in obedience to His word!

Just as God allowed the Israelites to see the Egyptians dead on the seashore, God may allow you to cross paths with people who were out to hurt you, who lied on you, who mistreated you, but it's not so that you can plan your revenge or give them a piece of your mind. It's so you can see how God brought you out of troubling situations, so you can give Him the glory for what He has done, and also realize that whatever it was they let the devil use them to launch at you is now a non-issue.

When the Israelites saw the dead Egyptians their faith went to another level. They were so happy most of chapter 15 is a song dedicated to God's victory over the Egyptians. When the morning comes for you and everything is much clearer, and you realize that God was working behind the scenes in your life to grant you victory in whatever your situation is, what is your song going to be?

Now that you see how God worked on behalf of the Israelites you should also know that God is not oblivious to your issue, and He can handle whatever that issue may be. I want you to take your focus off the issue, trust God completely, move forward, and start focusing on your victory song. Maybe your song is going to be about how God made a way for you out of no way. Maybe your song is going to be about how God brought you out of loneliness, depression, fear, sickness, abuse, financial hardship, grief, destructive habits, addictions, a bad relationship, and the list goes on. Maybe your song is about how God keeps providing for you day after day after day.

In his book, *Mere Christianity*, C.S. Lewis likened God's use of adversity to walking a dog. If the dog gets its leash wrapped around a pole, and tries to continue running forward, he will only tighten the leash more. Both the dog, and the owner are after the same end, forward motion, but the owner must resist the dog by pulling him opposite the direction he wants to go. The master, sharing the same intention, but understanding better than the dog where he really wants to go, takes an action precisely opposite to that of the dog's will. **It is in this way that God uses adversity**.

You will face situations that seem like you're not going to get out of, overcome, or get through. It may seem like defeat is a certainty and victory is not an option. Even in these situations, you can be victorious! How can we realize victory? By maintaining your faith in God. Keep your focus on Him. **You can never go wrong by maintaining your faith in God.** If God makes a promise He is more than able to fulfill it. Whatever it is, don't focus on the situation, understand that it's not what it looks like, and focus on the victory song because victory is yours!

Notes_____

_____

_____

_____

_____

_____

_____

_____

_____

_____

_____

_____

_____

_____

_____

_____

_____

_____

_____

_____

_____

Chapter 8

Maintaining Your Focus

In order to ensure your victory, you must know and speak the word. 2 Corinthians 4:13 says...

But having the same spirit of faith, according to what is written, "I BELIEVED, THEREFORE I SPOKE," we also believe, therefore we also speak,

Human nature wants to see and figure out everything before we can believe, and if we are not strong in faith, fear sets in. However, what is unseen is actually more reliable than that which is seen. This chapter is not an exhaustive exposition on the process of faith, but I believe it will help you maintain your focus. Here are some verses to take note of in your Bible...

2 Corinthians 4:18 says...

while we look not at the things which are seen, but at the things which are not seen; for the things which are seen are temporal, but the things which are not seen are eternal.

Hebrews 11:1-3 says...

Now faith is the assurance of things hoped for, the conviction of things not seen. For by it the men of old gained approval. By faith we understand that the worlds were prepared by the word of God, so that what is seen was not made out of things which are visible.

Finally, if we are not walking in faith and trusting God, we CANNOT please Him as shown in Hebrews 11:6...

And without faith it is impossible to please Him, for he who comes to God must believe that He is and that He is a rewarder of those who seek Him.

When it comes to faith, not knowing is knowing enough! What do I mean by saying not knowing is knowing enough? Simply put, you don't have to know how God is going to manifest His blessings in your life; you just need to know and believe that He will and then act like you know. We leave a lot of blessings on the table when we get gripped by fear and choose to do opposite of what God tells us to do. We fail to gain God's approval when we fail to walk by faith, not by sight. Hebrews 11:2 proves this point. We have to understand that there are two worlds. There is the physical world we can see, and the spiritual world we can't see. We must understand that it is not the physical world that we should rely on the most. We need to tap into the unseen spiritual dimension because the things which are not seen are preeminent and eternal and more reliable than the temporal things which we do see.

If God could call the universe into existence out of nothing that we can see, then isn't He able to provide for you if you exercise your faith in Him? My pastor, Bishop I.V. Hilliard, who I credit for giving me a clear understanding of the faith process, taught me just because something is not seen does not mean that it does not exist. You may not see the answer to your problem, you may not see your way out, you may not see how things are going to work out, but we have to rest in the fact that God already knows how He is going to bring you out! He already knows how He is going to bless you! If we don't obey His Word we basically are telling Him we don't think He is capable of honoring His Word to us. The fact of the matter is that God is not only able to fulfill His word, but He is able to do far beyond the unspeakable, unthinkable things Ephesians 3:20 says...

Now to Him who is able to do far more abundantly beyond all that we ask or think, according to the power that works within us,

Faith is to believe what we <u>do not see</u>; and the reward of this faith is to see what we believe. We need to exercise our faith! However, the question many people have is how do we exercise our faith?

We exercise our faith at least three ways...

1. We must believe.

Hebrews 11:6 says that without faith it is impossible to please God. It also says that he who comes to God must first believe that He is, and He is a rewarder of those that diligently seek Him. When someone is pleased with you it is synonymous with you gaining their approval. Therefore, we gain God's approval by having faith in Him. Hebrews 11:2 supports this. It says: *for by it the men of old gained approval.* By what? Hebrews 11:1 provides that answer. It was by faith. What does that mean?

- **By faith they believed in spite of what they saw therefore they were approved by God.**

- **By faith they trusted God even though there was no visible evidence to validate the sensibility of their trust, therefore they were approved.**

- **By faith they did not know how things would work out, but they had an assurance and conviction that God would be faithful to His word so they moved forward anyway. Therefore, they were approved.**

Also look at 1 Cor 10:13. As we walk by faith, we will always no doubt be tempted in various ways to do contrary to what faith requires. The temptation comes in various forms. When we fall to temptation and are unfaithful to God we are not pleasing Him. However, God is so gracious to us that even though He will allow the temptation He also provides the way of escape! What does that mean? He has put His Spirit in you and given you His Word to guide you, so the way of escape is simply having faith in Him and walking in obedience. A second way we exercise our faith and tap into the unseen provisions of God is...

2. We must give.

Malachi 3:8-10 says...

*"Will a man rob God? Yet you are robbing Me! But you say, 'How have we robbed You?' In tithes and offerings. You are cursed with a curse, for you are robbing Me, the whole nation of you! Bring the whole tithe into the storehouse, so that there may be food in My house, and test Me now in this," says the L*ORD *of hosts, "<u>if I will not open for you the windows of heaven and pour out for you a blessing until it overflows.</u>*

The tithe is only a beginning. It is just a start. We should AT LEAST tithe. We should do nothing less. Jesus confirms this in the New Testament in Matthew 23:23...

"Woe to you, scribes and Pharisees, hypocrites! For you tithe mint and dill and cummin, and have neglected the weightier provisions of the law: justice and mercy and faithfulness; but these are the things you should have done without neglecting the others.

Today tithing is the point from which we can tell how serious we are about honoring God and bringing glory to Jesus Christ. If we have not learned the joy of giving God's way, and that includes giving at least 10 percent of our income to God as we tithe in our local church, we have missed one of the greatest delights, privileges, and blessings that could ever be ours. In Luke 6:38 Jesus said...

"Give, and it shall be given unto you; good measure, pressed down, and shaken together, and running over, shall men give into your bosom. For with the same measure that ye mete withal it shall be measured to you again".

God is not a taker in any area; He is a giver in all areas. He will never allow himself to be indebted to us. The principle is this: If we want to receive, we must first prime the pump. If we want to receive, we must give. Jesus told us that if a man would save his life, he will lose it; but if he will lose his life for Christ's sake, he will find it. (Mark 8:35.) This is a principle of life. It is a principle that applies spiritually, materially, and financially. If we give according to God's principle, God will give back to us. The most dangerous thing in all the earth is to contradict one of the principles of God for our lives.

How many of you would go to a restaurant receive their service and the food they have provided and then leave without paying? More than likely you would not do that. You would pay the bill, because that is what belongs to them, and hopefully, you would leave a tip out of appreciation for what they have done. Why would we do that? Because it's simply right to do. It enables the establishment to continue doing business so that the next time you want to have a meal there you can. It enables them to pay salaries and to keep providing good food for your nourishment and enjoyment. If we won't fail to give in that situation (and you could use other scenarios such as the barber shop, beauty shop, nail salon, etc.) doesn't God deserve the same respect? When you come to the house of God you are fed the Word of God which increases your faith so that you can overcome any obstacles and challenges and live a victorious life in God. Your giving ensures that there is a place for you to come worship and hear the word and that the operating expenses are covered, that proper compensation is provided to those serving you and that ministry can go forth. Most importantly, we should give our tithes because just like the bill total belongs to the restaurant, the tithe belongs to God! If we don't tithe, the Bible calls us a God robber! We should give offerings because just like your tip shows appreciation for the service you received, your offering is a show of your gratitude to God. When we tithe the windows of Heaven are opened over our life and when we give our offering God is delighted because He loves a cheerful giver! **(Note: the tip is added to the bill. It does not stand alone. Likewise, your offering should not stand alone)**

The Apostle Paul uses the Christians of Macedonia as an example of those who have learned the blessed principle that it is more blessed to give than to receive. *"**Moreover, brethren, we do you to wit of the grace of God bestowed on the churches of Macedonia" (II Corinthians 8:1).*** All they did was give an offering. Yet the Bible declares that the grace of God was upon them. It allowed them to tap into the unseen provision of God. They were experiencing "bad times" in a great trial of affliction **as they gave**. (READ II Corinthians 8:2.) Those things do not go together in our rational thinking. They gave and the grace of God was bestowed upon them. Even though they were afflicted, they had an abundance of joy that abounded unto the riches of their liberality. The Macedonian believers begged for the privilege of giving. (READ II Corinthians 8:3.) God honors His Word. These Macedonians did not stop to figure up how much they needed for next week. They said, "Please give us a chance to make a gift." They had learned a secret. They had learned that they were cheating themselves if they did not give. They had also learned that giving is a blessed principle. Some people say they cannot afford to tithe. The truth is that we cannot afford not to tithe. As we give, we access the unseen provisions of God, and God blesses us more than we could ever imagine. The real tragedy comes when we withhold from God. God asserts to us that if we will do things His way, we will be blessed. If we will not do things as He has instructed us, we will only harm ourselves.

3. We must speak. (2 Corinthians 4:13; 2 Corinthians 4:18; Proverbs 18:20)

Read 2 Corinthians 4:13. This verse is a direct reference to Psalm 116:10. I like how Psalm 116:10 is expounded upon in the Amplified Bible. It says *I believed (trusted in, relied on, and clung to my God), and therefore have I spoken [even when I said], I am greatly afflicted.* So regardless how your situation may look, speak God's word over it and continue to expect God's blessing to manifest.

Fear blocks our access to the unseen things. There are things that God would do in your life, but your fear will not authorize you to walk into those blessings. If we are not operating by faith, we are operating by fear. Fear is not of God! Paul told Timothy in 2 Timothy 1:7 *God has not given us a Spirit of Fear but of power, love and a sound mind.* Timothy was young and some believers and nonbelievers were questioning his leadership. He was ready to call it quits! He was probably getting intimidated by the reaction of the people, but Paul was encouraging him to be bold. When people know what they need to be doing for God but they aren't, it is fear that is behind it. What we tend to do is appease our conscience and say, I'm praying about it, when in fact, God has already given the verdict and is waiting on us! When we are in fear we expect something negative to happen. However, if we have faith in God we should expect something positive! Romans 8:28 tells us…

And we know that God causes all things to work together for good to those who love God, to those who are called according to His purpose.

When we are operating by fear, we look at our situation and size it up and based on our assessment, we rule out the possibility of God being able to fulfill His promise to us. It is reported that the newspaper counselor, Ann Landers, receives an average of 10,000 letters each month, and nearly all of them from people burdened with problems. She was asked if there was any one of them which predominates throughout the letters she receives, and her reply was the one problem above all others seems to be fear. People are afraid of losing their health, their wealth, and their loved ones. People are afraid of life itself.

When we walk by faith and trust God we are granted a peace that passes all understanding. We must maintain a reliance on the unseen, supernatural realm. How do we do that? Drop your anchor in faith and start confessing what you are in God! When an anchor is dropped it goes into an area that is unseen to you from the surface. You have to trust that it is latched on to something that will keep you in place, but you can't see it. You can see the effects of the wind that may blow, and you can see the effects of the waves as they roll, but if you are anchored, you will not be overcome! **Make the choice to walk by faith and not fear.** I found out that you DO NOT have to be in fear. Fear is not driven by circumstance; it is a choice you make. You choose to be in fear just like you choose to walk by faith Let's look at an example in 2 Kings 6:15-18 which says…

Now when the attendant of the man of God had risen early and gone out, behold, an army with horses and chariots was circling the city. And his servant said to him, "Alas, my master! What shall we do?" So he answered, "Do not fear, for those who are with us are more than those who are with them." Then Elisha prayed and said, "O LORD, I pray, open his eyes that he may see." And the LORD opened the servant's eyes and he saw; and behold, the mountain was full of horses and chariots of fire all around Elisha. When they came down to him, Elisha prayed to the LORD and said, "Strike this people with blindness, I pray." So He struck them with blindness according to the word of Elisha.

In 2 Kings 6:15-18 we have two different perspectives of the same event. The servant was afraid. Elisha was not moved. It is reasonable to think that Elisha may have had an initial reaction of fear, but that quickly transitioned to faith. Why wasn't Elisha as fearful as the servant?

- **Because of His faith, he <u>chose</u> not to be fearful even though the evidence he saw said they were outnumbered. (Faith is the substance of things hoped for and evidence of things NOT seen)**

- **Because of this faith, God gave Him the vision to see something in the Spirit realm that gave birth to his words that probably made no sense initially to his servant. (If the enemy knew what he saw they probably would not have attempted to attack)**

- **Because of His faith he prayed and asked God to open his servant's eyes that he could also see. (it helps to get with people who are strong in faith)**

- **Because of faith, the enemy attack was nullified.**

I could say so much more about this story, but it reminds me of a story I read that said, the degree of faith that one places in a given object is directly proportional to one's knowledge of the object. For example, consider a man terrified of flying. When he first arrives at an airport he buys insurance at those coin-operated insurance-policy machines. He has his seat belt buckled twenty minutes before take-off and is sure to listen carefully to the routine "emergency in-structions." He has no faith in the ability of the plane to get him to his destination. But, as the journey progresses, this passenger begins to change. He first unbuckles his seat belt, then has some lunch, and pretty soon is talking to the person next to him and joking. Why the change? What happened? Is there more faith at 36,000 feet? Of course not. The more he learned about the object of faith, the plane, the more faith he exercised in that object. So it is with believers. The more we learn of the Lord, the more faith we can place in him.

Notes_____

_____

_____

_____

_____

_____

_____

_____

_____

_____

_____

_____

_____

_____

_____

_____

_____

_____

_____

_____

_____

Chapter 9

A Final Word of Encouragement

Even when it seems life has dealt you a knockout blow, as the old saying goes, it's not over until it's over! As it pertains to you, the child of God, you plus God is **ALWAYS**, the majority. God is able to see you through situations that would defeat others, but because of your relationship with Him, and faith in His word, you won't throw in the towel as soon as you are dealt what seems to be a knockout blow. Maybe you lost a loved one, a job, or a business venture went awry. Maybe you have been in an abusive relationship, divorced, experienced depression or low self-esteem. Maybe you are in a situation right now as you are reading this, that seems like it is going to take you out. I say to you, be encouraged, God has not forgotten you. Keep praying, keep being faithful in your church, keep applying the word to your life and watch how God shows up for you.

Sometimes doubt may creep in, but don't let that cause you to quit. There is a story told in the bible about a man that came to Jesus because his son had a spirit that needed to be cast out, He took the boy to the disciples and they could do nothing. Jesus told the man, if he could believe, all things were possible. The man immediately cried out, Lord I believe, help thou my unbelief! In other words, he believed that Jesus was able to help him even if his mind couldn't figure out how! He went to Jesus with an expectation of things working out for his son, even though in his mind he couldn't figure out how it was going to happen.

I remember SO MANY times in my life when my wife and I had to exercise faith, even when we couldn't figure out how God was going to work things out. For example, when the Lord told me to move my family to Round Rock, TX, just outside Austin, and I told my family and we took the step of faith, it seemed like all the forces of darkness mobilized to stop what God had told me to do. We found a neighborhood we liked, started building a house, and then I was laid off from my job.

We could have told the builder of our home that we could no longer afford to build the house, and we could have called off starting the ministry altogether, but we continued walking in the spirit and did not ful ill the desires of the flesh! When you operate in faith, you are not moved by what you see! You may have doubt in your head, and can't figure out how God is going to do what He said, but you remain in faith and watch God bring the results to pass!

My wife and I have talked about writing a book together in the future, on the many, many testimonies of how God brought us through, just like He did with the Israelites and others in scripture, but I pray that as a result of reading this book, you will move you forward in faith, trust God regardless of how things look, speak His word over every situation, and see the manifestation of His promises as you remain focused in faith. It's not what it looks like, and you will see if you don't quit! Your blessing is on the way!!!

Notes_____

_____

_____

_____

_____

_____

_____

_____

_____

_____

_____

_____

_____

_____

_____

_____

_____

_____

_____

_____

_____

About the Author

Bishop Calvin M. Hooper is the Pastor of the Household of Faith Christian Fellowship Church, founded by he and his wife Pastor Valerie Hooper in 2003 along with their five children. The church has a vision for locations in multiple states.

The More Like Him radio broadcast is a ministry they started which broadcasts on several stations of the Wilkins Radio Network. They can currently be heard on stations in California, Kansas, Missouri, and Florida, with plans to expand to all 23 stations of the network. They also stream their services live internationally every week.

Bishop Hooper is the author of three other books, Walk the Walk, 8 Essentials for Following Jesus (Destiny Image Publishers), and Respect Yourself: Becoming the Woman God Made You to Be, and many more titles are forthcoming. He is a decorated military veteran, voice over artist, and the Co-Founder of Living Faith Publications along with his wife Pastor Valerie.

LIVING FAITH
PUBLICATIONS.

P.O. Box 5056

Round Rock, TX 78683

Household of Faith

Christian Fellowship Church, Inc

The teaching ministry of

Bishop Calvin and Pastor Valerie Hooper

www.thehouseonline.org

Copies of this resource can be ordered by going to:

amazon.com/author/calvinhooper

www.ingramcontent.com/pod-product-compliance
Lightning Source LLC
Chambersburg PA
CBHW060158070426
42447CB00033B/2201